Leveling Up Your Private Practice:

A Guide to Success for Therapists & Psych NPs

Georgina Twumasi

APRN, Psychiatric APRN

Print ISBN: **978-1-966491-35-4**

Ebook ISBN: **978-1-966491-36-1**

Audiobook ISBN: **978-1-966491-37-8**

Printed in the United States of America

Story Corner Publishing & Consulting, Inc.

Chesapeake, VA 23321

Storycornerpublishing@yahoo.com

www.StoryCornerPublishing.com

Table of Contents

Introduction

Overview of Private Practice Challenges and Opportunities

Launching or growing a private practice is one of the most empowering decisions a therapist can make. It represents freedom — the freedom to shape your clinical identity, set your own schedule, and serve clients in a way that truly aligns with your values. Yet, with that freedom comes a unique set of challenges that few clinicians are fully prepared for.

Many of us entered the mental health field to heal, serve, and empower others, not necessarily to run a business. Graduate school equipped us with diagnostic skills, clinical interventions, and ethical principles, but rarely did it teach us how to manage marketing budgets, navigate insurance contracts, or set boundaries with clients. This lack of business training can make private practice feel overwhelming at times.

From choosing the right fee structure to managing cancellations, many clinicians find themselves stuck in a constant cycle of helping others while neglecting their own financial well-being. As a result, burnout becomes a silent threat, and the joy of private practice can fade beneath administrative stress and inconsistent income.

However, private practice is also a space of incredible opportunity. It allows you to:

- Craft a professional identity that reflects your authenticity
- Build financial independence through fair pricing and efficient systems

- Create deeper therapeutic relationships without the limits of rigid agency models
- Offer specialized services that meet your clients' unique needs
- Develop multiple income streams (courses, workshops, consulting, or group practice)

The goal of this guide is to help you not only survive in private practice — but thrive in it. Because success in private practice isn't just about filling your calendar; it's about creating sustainable systems that honor your time, value, and mental health.

*****

The Heart Behind Private Practice

Before diving into business strategies, it's important to remember why you started this journey.

For most therapists, the call to private practice stems from a deeper desire — the desire to serve authentically and to provide care without the bureaucracy of larger institutions. You may have felt limited by insurance constraints, high caseloads, or environments that prioritized productivity over people.

Private practice offers you the chance to redefine success. It invites you to merge clinical excellence with entrepreneurial confidence, creating a practice that reflects your vision of healing, balance, and freedom.

But that requires more than clinical skill — it requires a mindset shift.

You are not "just a therapist."

You are also a business owner, strategist, and visionary.

You are responsible not only for your clients' growth but also for your own professional evolution.

*****

Common Pitfalls for New and Growing Practitioners

Even the most skilled clinicians can struggle when transitioning into business ownership. Some common challenges include:

1. Undercharging and Overgiving – Many therapists fear that raising prices will drive clients away. This often leads to resentment, exhaustion, and financial instability.
2. Poor Boundaries – Without firm policies around scheduling, communication, and cancellations, your time and energy can quickly become depleted.
3. Inconsistent Marketing – Relying solely on word-of-mouth or directory listings limits growth potential. A lack of visibility means fewer opportunities to connect with your ideal clients.
4. Neglecting Self-Care – Running a practice is emotionally and mentally demanding. Without intentional rest and structure, burnout is inevitable.
5. Fear of the Business Side – Many therapists feel uneasy with terms like "sales," "profit," or "marketing," believing they conflict with compassion. In reality, understanding business principles strengthens your ability to serve sustainably.

Recognizing these pitfalls is the first step toward overcoming them. Each subsequent chapter in this book will provide practical strategies and mindset shifts to help you build a thriving, values-driven practice.

*****

Reframing Success in Private Practice

Success in private practice isn't defined by how many clients you see or how much money you make — it's about alignment.

Are your systems working for you or against you?

Does your schedule reflect the life you want to live?

Do you feel energized by your work, or drained by constant demands?

When your practice is aligned with your purpose, your business becomes an extension of your calling, not a burden.

That alignment begins when you:

- Set clear boundaries
- Charge appropriately for your expertise
- Build systems that reduce stress
- Invest in marketing that amplifies your mission
- Cultivate relationships with clients built on trust and communication

True success means your practice thrives and you do too.

*****

The Purpose of This Guide

This book was written to help therapists like you step into their full potential — both as clinicians and entrepreneurs. It's a roadmap to building a sustainable, ethical, and profitable practice without compromising your integrity or compassion.

By the end of this guide, you will:

- Understand your worth and feel confident in your pricing
- Establish strong boundaries with no-show and cancellation policies
- Develop marketing strategies that attract the right clients
- Engage and retain clients through intentional communication
- Fill your caseload with clients who value your expertise
- Trust the process of business growth and clinical evolution

Each chapter will blend practical business advice with emotional and psychological insights — because being a successful therapist in private practice is as much about mindset as it is about management.

*****

A Final Word: Your Journey Starts Here

As you begin this book, remember that building your private practice is a journey, not a race. There will be moments of clarity and moments of doubt. You may have months that are fully booked and others that feel uncertain. But every challenge is a teacher — and every step forward, no matter how small, is progress.

You already have what it takes to build a thriving practice.

What you may need now is guidance, structure, and confidence to take bold, consistent action.

This guide is your companion on that journey — a resource to remind you that success in private practice isn't reserved for the few. It's available to every therapist willing to believe in their value, do the work, and trust the process.

"You are not just running a business — you are building a legacy of healing, one client at a time."

— Georgina Twumasi, APRN, Psychiatric APRN

Chapter 1:

Charging Your Worth

The Truth About Worth and Wealth in Private Practice

Let's start with a truth many therapists struggle to accept:

You deserve to be well-compensated for the life-changing work you do.

Charging your worth isn't about greed — it's about alignment. It's about honoring your time, your education, your energy, and the emotional labor that comes with helping others heal. It's also about setting a financial foundation that allows you to serve from a place of abundance, not burnout.

As therapists, nurses, and healers, we often internalize the message that caring professions should be driven purely by compassion — not financial gain. While compassion is the heart of what we do, it should never come at the cost of your own stability or peace of mind.

You can care deeply and charge confidently. The two are not mutually exclusive.

When you charge your worth, you model self-respect, boundaries, and empowerment — the very principles you teach your clients.

*****

Emotional Reasons Behind Undercharging

Most therapists don't undercharge because they lack skill — they undercharge because they doubt their value. This emotional conflict is deeply rooted in fear and internalized beliefs.

1. Fear of Rejection

Many clinicians believe that if they charge too much, clients will leave or new ones won't come. This fear stems from a scarcity mindset — the idea that there aren't enough clients or opportunities to go around.

But the truth is, there's no shortage of people who need help. When you charge your worth, you attract clients who value and respect your expertise.

2. Guilt Around Making Money

Some therapists feel guilty profiting from others' pain. But therapy isn't about exploitation — it's about transformation. And transformation requires investment.

Clients are more likely to commit to their growth when they make a financial investment in the process. Paying for therapy is part of the healing journey — it reinforces accountability and value.

3. Imposter Syndrome

Even highly qualified professionals experience self-doubt. "Who am I to charge that much?" or "What if I'm not experienced enough?"

Imposter syndrome whispers lies that you're not ready, even when you are. Remember — your degree, license, experience, and empathy are evidence of your worth. Your value doesn't depend on comparison to others but on the impact you create.

4. People-Pleasing Tendencies

Therapists are natural nurturers. We want to help, fix, and ease burdens — even at our own expense. People-pleasing can lead you to compromise your financial boundaries to avoid conflict or discomfort. But constantly accommodating others' financial limitations only drains you and diminishes your practice's stability.

*****

Lack of Financial Education

Let's be honest — most mental health training programs teach almost nothing about running a business. We learn to document, diagnose, and treat — but not to bill, budget, or build wealth. This gap in financial education keeps many clinicians in a cycle of survival rather than success.

Without clear financial systems, it's easy to:

- Undervalue sessions or services
- Fail to track expenses and profit margins
- Feel lost when calculating break-even points
- Struggle to budget for taxes, retirement, or growth investments

But knowledge is power. Once you understand the numbers behind your worth, confidence follows naturally.

Here's a simple framework to start:

The "Worth Calculation"

1. Determine Your Ideal Monthly Income — Include taxes, savings, business expenses, and your desired take-home pay.
2. Calculate Your Available Clinical Hours — Be realistic about how many sessions you can handle weekly without burnout.
3. Divide Income by Hours — This gives you the minimum rate you need to charge per session to meet your financial goals.

For example, if your goal is $10,000 per month and you can comfortably see 20 clients a week (80 per month), your base rate should be $125 per session minimum — before accounting for growth, continuing education, or reinvestment.

When you know your numbers, you take emotion out of the equation and make informed, empowered decisions.

*****

Cultural and Gender Stigmas

Money beliefs are often inherited — passed down through culture, religion, gender expectations, or upbringing.

Many clinicians, especially women and people of color, have been socialized to:

- Put others first
- Avoid discussing money

- Equate modesty with virtue
- Believe financial success is incompatible with humility or service

These subconscious scripts can create guilt or shame around setting high fees or increasing rates. But breaking generational cycles of financial limitation is also a form of healing.

When you claim your worth, you create a new narrative — one that says it's okay to serve and succeed.

It's okay to make money doing meaningful work.

It's okay to want stability, freedom, and abundance.

*****

Steps to Overcome These Challenges

1. Redefine Your Relationship With Money

Money is not evil or corrupt; it's a tool. The more you have, the more impact you can make. Money in the hands of heart-centered professionals creates ripple effects of healing and empowerment.

Try affirmations like:

- "My work changes lives, and I deserve to be compensated accordingly."
- "Charging my worth allows me to serve at a higher level."
- "Abundance flows where purpose and preparation meet."

2. Anchor Your Fees in Logic, Not Emotion

Instead of thinking, "What can my clients afford?" ask, "What does my practice need to thrive?"

Establish your rates based on the value of your services, your training, and your financial goals — not on guilt or comparison.

3. Communicate Your Value Clearly

When clients understand the value and transformation you provide, they focus less on price and more on results.

For example:

"My role is to help you move from surviving to thriving — to create lasting change, not just temporary relief. My rate reflects my training, experience, and commitment to your growth."

4. Set and Hold Financial Boundaries

Have a clear payment policy that includes rates, due dates, and cancellation rules. Enforce it consistently and professionally. Boundaries protect both you and your clients.

5. Normalize Rate Increases

Your fees should grow with your expertise, inflation, and demand. Reassess every 6–12 months. Announce increases respectfully but confidently. Example:

"Beginning January 1st, my session rate will increase to reflect my continued professional development and the quality of care I provide."

6. Get Comfortable Talking About Money

Avoid apologizing when stating your rates. Speak calmly, directly, and without justification.

Example:

"My session rate is $150. I accept self-pay and offer invoices for reimbursement. Would you like me to send you the intake paperwork?"

Confidence builds trust. Clients sense when you believe in your value.

*****

A Note on Accessibility and Compassion

Charging your worth doesn't mean turning away clients in need. You can still maintain compassion while running a sustainable practice. Consider:

- Offering a limited number of sliding-scale spots
- Partnering with community organizations or nonprofits for pro bono work
- Providing group sessions or workshops for affordability

The key is balance. You can serve underserved communities without sacrificing your own stability.

Remember: A drained therapist cannot pour into others. A thriving therapist can.

*****

Practical Exercise: Reclaiming Your Worth

Take a moment to reflect and write:

1. What beliefs did I grow up with about money and service?
2. How have those beliefs influenced how I set my fees?
3. What would it feel like to charge a rate that truly reflects my value?
4. What would I be able to do — personally and professionally — if my income increased by 25% this year?

Reflect on your answers without judgment. Awareness is the first step toward transformation.

*****

Key Takeaway

Charging your worth isn't just about numbers — it's about identity.

It's about choosing to see yourself not only as a therapist but as a professional, expert, and entrepreneur.

When you confidently stand in your worth, you give clients permission to do the same in their own lives.

"The moment you start valuing your work, the world will too."

— Georgina Twumasi, APRN, Psychiatric APRN

Chapter 2:

No Show Policy in Private Practice

Valuing Your Time as a Therapist

Your time is sacred. Every appointment slot represents not just income, but emotional energy, preparation, and opportunity. When a client fails to show up or cancels last minute, it's not just an inconvenience — it's a disruption that affects your schedule, your other clients, and your peace of mind.

Many therapists hesitate to enforce no-show or cancellation fees because they fear appearing harsh, unempathetic, or "money-hungry." However, setting clear expectations is not unkind — it's a form of professional self-respect and an important model of healthy boundaries for your clients.

A consistent no-show policy says, "I respect my time, and I respect yours."

It communicates reliability, structure, and accountability — all of which are essential to therapeutic success.

Remember: enforcing a policy doesn't diminish your compassion; it protects your ability to continue providing care.

*****

The Importance of Valuing Your Time

As a clinician, you're in the business of emotional labor — and that labor has value. When a client misses an appointment, you lose:

- The billable hour
- The chance to help another client in need
- The energy and focus you allocated for that session

Repeated no-shows can quickly add up to significant lost income. For example, if your session rate is $150 and you experience just three no-shows a month, that's $5,400 a year in lost revenue — not counting the emotional toll of constant disruptions.

Your time is not replaceable. When clients understand that, they are more likely to take their sessions seriously.

*****

Establishing and Communicating a No-Show Policy

Your policy should be clear, consistent, and communicated from the very first interaction. Most scheduling problems arise not from malice, but from miscommunication or unclear expectations.

Step 1: Define Your Policy

A standard, professional policy should include:

- Required notice period (typically 24 to 48 hours) for cancellations

- Full session fee or partial fee charged for late cancellations or no-shows
- Acceptable forms of notice (email, phone, client portal, etc.)
- How emergencies are handled (discretionary exceptions)

Example Policy:

Cancellations and No-Shows:

Because your appointment time is reserved exclusively for you, a 24-hour notice is required for cancellations. Appointments canceled with less than 24-hour notice or missed without notice will be charged the full session fee. Exceptions may be made in the case of emergencies at the therapist's discretion.

This language is clear, kind, and professional — and it balances compassion with accountability.

*****

Step 2: Include It in Writing

Your no-show policy should appear in:

- Your informed consent documents
- Your client intake forms
- Your practice website and scheduling software

Having it in writing eliminates confusion and helps you enforce it confidently. During the first session, briefly review the policy out loud with clients.

Example Script:

"Before we get started, I just want to review my cancellation policy. I ask for at least 24 hours' notice if you need to cancel or reschedule. If a session is missed or canceled late, the full session fee applies. I do make exceptions for true emergencies — I just ask that you communicate as soon as possible. Does that sound fair?"

This sets expectations early and prevents misunderstandings later.

*****

Step 3: Enforce It Consistently

The hardest part of any boundary is holding it. Many therapists feel tempted to waive fees or make exceptions for fear of losing clients. However, inconsistency creates confusion and resentment — both for you and your clients.

When you enforce your policy consistently, clients learn to respect your time. They also internalize an important therapeutic principle: boundaries build trust.

If you repeatedly waive your policy, you unintentionally teach clients that your time — and by extension, their commitment — doesn't matter. But when you follow through respectfully, you model accountability, which can become part of their growth.

*****

Handling Client Communication Around No-Shows

How you communicate after a missed session can make all the difference. The goal is to uphold your boundary while maintaining rapport and professionalism.

Scenario 1: Missed Appointment, No Contact

Send a brief, nonjudgmental message the same day.

Example Email or Text:

"Hi [Client Name], I noticed we missed our session today. I hope you're doing okay. Per my cancellation policy, the full session fee will be applied for missed appointments without notice. Please let me know if you'd like to reschedule for next week."

This message is warm yet firm — it conveys care without compromising policy.

*****

Scenario 2: Client Apologizes After Missing

Example Response:

"Thank you for reaching out, [Client Name]. I completely understand that life happens. However, because that appointment time was reserved exclusively for you, the no-show fee still applies. I'm looking forward to continuing our work together next session."

This reinforces boundaries while preserving the therapeutic alliance.

*****

Scenario 3: Chronic No-Shows or Late Cancellations

If a pattern develops, it's important to address it therapeutically — not just administratively. Chronic lateness or absence often reflects deeper issues like avoidance, anxiety, or ambivalence about change.

Example Conversation:

"I've noticed it's been difficult for you to attend consistently. I want to explore what's getting in the way. Consistency is key to your progress, and when sessions are missed, it impacts your growth and our ability to meet your goals. How can we address this together?"

Approaching it from a place of curiosity keeps the conversation constructive while still emphasizing accountability.

*****

Using Technology to Support Your Policy

Modern tools can help minimize no-shows:

- Automated reminders: Send appointment texts or emails 24 hours in advance.

- Online scheduling systems: Require a credit card on file for easy billing.
- Client portals: Allow rescheduling or cancellation within policy limits.

These systems save time, prevent misunderstandings, and reduce emotional labor.

*****

Balancing Compassion and Professionalism

Boundaries do not mean rigidity. Flexibility within reason shows empathy, especially during emergencies or unexpected hardships. However, flexibility should never compromise your sustainability.

When deciding whether to waive a fee, ask:

1. Is this a one-time emergency or a recurring pattern?
2. Does making an exception here support or harm the therapeutic relationship?
3. Am I making this choice from compassion — or from guilt or fear of client loss?

Trust your professional judgment, not emotion. You can always show kindness without abandoning boundaries.

*****

Modeling Healthy Boundaries for Clients

Clients learn through observation. By maintaining and communicating your policies with confidence and respect, you teach them that:

- Boundaries are a form of self-care.
- Accountability is a part of growth.
- Mutual respect strengthens relationships.

For clients who struggle with boundaries in their own lives, your consistency becomes a living example of emotional health. They see that honoring commitments is both empowering and healing.

In other words, your no-show policy isn't just a business practice — it's a therapeutic tool.

*****

Reframing the Policy as Partnership

It's helpful to frame your no-show policy not as a punishment, but as a partnership. You are not enforcing a rule against your client — you are protecting the space for them.

You might say:

"This policy helps ensure that I can reserve the time and energy needed to fully show up for you and all of my clients. It's part of maintaining a healthy, reliable therapeutic environment."

This reframing transforms the policy into a shared value — reliability — rather than a one-sided rule.

*****

Practical Steps for Implementation

1. Write and Review: Create a clearly worded policy. Review it with each new client.
2. Automate Reminders: Use scheduling software to minimize no-shows.
3. Document in Intake: Have clients sign acknowledgment forms.
4. Communicate Kindly: Address missed sessions promptly and professionally.
5. Stay Consistent: Apply the same standards to every client.
6. Reflect Periodically: Review your policy annually to ensure it still aligns with your workflow and boundaries.

*****

Key Takeaway

Your no-show policy is a reflection of your professional integrity. It protects your time, your energy, and your financial health — while teaching clients that structure and respect are part of healing.

Boundaries don't block connection; they create safety. And safety —
both emotional and professional — is where true transformation begins.

"When you respect your time, you teach others to do the same."

— Georgina Twumasi, APRN, Psychiatric APRN

Chapter 3:

Marketing Your Private Practice

Understanding Your Value

One of the most common barriers that therapists face when it comes to marketing is the belief that "helping people" and "promoting oneself" don't belong in the same sentence. Many clinicians associate marketing with salesmanship, manipulation, or self-promotion. But the truth is, marketing is about connection—sharing your gifts with the people who need them most.

Your value as a therapist extends far beyond your session rate. It's rooted in the transformation you help your clients achieve—the relief, growth, and healing they experience under your care. When you understand and embrace the impact of your work, you begin to see marketing not as a chore, but as a ministry of awareness. You're letting potential clients know that help is available, and that it's okay to take the next step toward healing.

Ask yourself:

- What transformation do my clients experience after working with me?
- What specific pain points or struggles do I help them overcome?
- What makes my therapeutic approach unique?

When you clearly define your value, it becomes much easier to communicate it to others—whether through your website, social media, or word-of-mouth.

*****

Overcoming Fear of Investment in Marketing

Many private practice owners hesitate to invest money into marketing, especially when just starting out. The fear often sounds like: "What if I don't get a return?" or "I can't afford this right now."

However, the truth is, you can't afford not to invest. Marketing is not an expense—it's an investment in visibility, credibility, and sustainability.

Think of marketing as planting seeds. Some will sprout immediately; others will take time. The more intentional and consistent you are, the more your practice will grow. Start small if needed—allocate a monthly marketing budget and increase it as your client load and income expand.

Investing in marketing may look like:

- Building a professional website optimized for client conversion.
- Running targeted ads on Google or social media.
- Hiring a copywriter to help articulate your message clearly.
- Investing in professional headshots and branding materials.
- Attending networking events or sponsoring local community programs.

When you view marketing as a long-term growth strategy rather than a one-time expense, you start to build momentum that compounds over time.

*****

Creating a Unique Brand

Your brand is more than just your logo or color palette—it's the essence of who you are as a therapist and what clients can expect when they work with you. A strong brand communicates your values, your voice, and your vision. It sets you apart from others in the industry.

To develop your brand, reflect on:

- Your mission: Why do you do what you do?
- Your niche: Who do you help, and how?
- Your personality: What makes you relatable and trustworthy?
- Your tone: Are you formal and clinical, or warm and conversational?

Once you have clarity on your brand identity, ensure that every piece of communication reflects it—your website, emails, business cards, social media posts, and even your therapy room ambiance. Consistency across all touchpoints builds trust and familiarity.

Remember: People don't just buy services—they buy connection and confidence. Your brand helps create that connection before a client ever books a session.

*****

Effective Marketing Strategies

Now that you've built the foundation, it's time to take action. Here are several effective marketing strategies for private practice therapists:

1. Build a Strong Online Presence:

    Your website is your digital office. It should be professional, welcoming, and easy to navigate. Include a bio that reflects your warmth and expertise, a clear list of services, and an easy way for clients to contact or book you.

2. Use Social Media Wisely:

    Platforms like Instagram, Facebook, TikTok, and LinkedIn can help you reach potential clients and build your professional authority. Share bite-sized insights, mental health tips, and behind-the-scenes glimpses of your practice. Be consistent, authentic, and educational.

3. Leverage Google Business and Directories:

    Claim your Google Business Profile and get listed in directories such as Psychology Today, TherapyDen, or Zencare. These platforms drive organic traffic and make it easier for clients in your area to find you.

4. Content Marketing:

    Consider blogging, podcasting, or creating videos that address common mental health topics. Offering value upfront helps establish you as a trusted expert, which naturally leads to more inquiries.

5. Email Marketing:

Build an email list of interested clients and colleagues. Send regular newsletters with helpful resources, practice updates, and words of encouragement. Staying top-of-mind ensures that when someone needs help, they'll think of you first.

6. Networking and Collaborations:

Build relationships with physicians, schools, churches, and community organizations. Host workshops or webinars. Word-of-mouth remains one of the strongest marketing tools in mental health care.

*****

The Importance of Consistency in Marketing Efforts

Marketing success doesn't happen overnight. The therapists who thrive in private practice are the ones who show up consistently—sharing their message, refining their brand, and nurturing their audience.

Set aside time each week for marketing activities. Treat it as a non-negotiable appointment in your business. Whether it's writing a blog, posting on social media, or following up with potential referral partners, consistency keeps your momentum strong.

Remember: Consistency builds credibility, and credibility builds clients.

The clients you help today may have first encountered you months—or even years—ago. Your consistent presence reminds them that you're still here, ready to help when they're ready to take that next step.

*****

Final Thoughts

Marketing your private practice doesn't have to feel overwhelming or "salesy." It's about sharing your passion and purpose in a way that resonates with the people you're meant to serve. When you understand your value, embrace investment, and remain consistent, your marketing efforts will begin to yield not only financial rewards but also deeper fulfillment and a lasting impact in the lives of your clients.

Chapter 4:

Client Engagement Strategies

A thriving private practice isn't built on marketing alone—it's sustained by meaningful, lasting relationships with clients. Engagement is the heartbeat of your practice. It's what turns a one-time visitor into a committed, returning client who feels valued, heard, and supported.

Client engagement goes far beyond the initial intake session; it's an ongoing process that begins before your first meeting and continues long after a client completes therapy. The more intentional you are about nurturing those relationships, the more trust and loyalty you'll build, leading to stronger outcomes and more referrals.

*****

Building Strong Client Relationships

At the core of every successful therapeutic relationship is trust. Clients must feel emotionally safe, respected, and understood. They are not just seeking a professional—they are seeking a human connection with someone who truly cares about their healing journey.

Here are ways to cultivate strong client relationships:

1. Be Fully Present.

    Your presence is your power. When clients sense that you are genuinely attentive—listening, not just hearing—they feel valued. Silence your phone, maintain eye contact, and create a calm, distraction-free environment that says, "You have my full attention."

2. Show Empathy, Not Just Sympathy.

    Empathy bridges the gap between professional expertise and human understanding. It tells clients, "I see you, and I understand." Reflective statements like, "It sounds like you felt invisible in that moment," can deepen trust and openness.

3. Celebrate Small Wins.

    Therapy is not only about addressing problems; it's also about acknowledging progress. Celebrating even minor breakthroughs motivates clients and reinforces their belief in the process.

4. Personalize the Experience.

    Remember details about your clients' lives—birthdays, milestones, or major transitions. Personalized touches such as a congratulatory note or a simple "checking in" message can make a world of difference.

Strong relationships don't happen by chance—they're cultivated through consistent empathy, professionalism, and genuine care.

*****

The Role of Communication in Engagement

Effective communication is the backbone of client engagement. It's not just about what you say, but how, when, and why you say it. Good communication strengthens the therapeutic alliance, prevents misunderstandings, and keeps clients invested in their treatment.

1. Clear and Transparent Expectations

From the first consultation, communicate your practice policies, fees, and boundaries clearly. Ambiguity breeds confusion, which can erode trust. Clients appreciate knowing what to expect and how the process works.

2. Consistent Check-Ins

Regularly check in with clients about how they feel the sessions are going. You can ask,

"What has been most helpful for you so far?"

"Is there anything you'd like to focus more on next session?"

This empowers clients to take ownership of their growth and ensures they feel heard.

3. Tone and Delivery

Your tone communicates as much as your words. Maintain a calm, supportive, and confident demeanor that reassures clients, especially when addressing sensitive or challenging topics.

4. Timely Responses

Whether it's an email, voicemail, or portal message, respond in a timely and respectful manner. Even a brief acknowledgment ("I received your message and will respond by tomorrow") shows attentiveness and professionalism.

5. Use of Technology

Consider secure client portals, automated appointment reminders, or telehealth check-ins to maintain communication between sessions. These tools make clients feel cared for and help reduce no-shows.

*****

Tools and Techniques for Client Retention

Keeping clients engaged long-term isn't just about providing quality therapy—it's about creating a seamless, supportive experience from beginning to end. Here are practical tools and techniques that encourage retention:

1. Client Portals and Apps

   Use HIPAA-compliant platforms where clients can easily schedule sessions, access notes, or complete forms. Convenience increases satisfaction.

2. Progress Tracking Tools

   Incorporate mood charts, journaling templates, or progress scales. When clients can visualize their growth, it reinforces motivation and accountability.

3. Therapeutic Homework

Assign practical, achievable exercises that extend learning between sessions. For example, mindfulness logs, gratitude journals, or boundary-setting worksheets keep clients actively engaged in their healing process.

4. Client Feedback Surveys

Send periodic satisfaction surveys to evaluate what's working and what isn't. Constructive feedback helps you refine your services and shows clients that their input matters.

5. Follow-Up After Major Breakthroughs or Gaps

Send a thoughtful message after a meaningful session or if a client hasn't booked in a while:

"I've been thinking about our last session and the progress you made. How are you feeling this week?"

These gestures build rapport and demonstrate genuine investment in their well-being.

6. Offer Packages or Membership Options

Instead of single sessions, offer structured programs or session bundles. This provides a sense of commitment and helps clients view therapy as a continuous journey rather than a sporadic service.

*****

Maintaining Regular Follow-Up with Clients

The work doesn't end when the session does. Regular follow-up shows clients that you are committed to their continued success, not just the billable hour. Follow-ups also provide an opportunity to check in, reinforce growth, and reopen communication with clients who may have paused therapy.

Strategies for Meaningful Follow-Up:

- Post-Treatment Check-Ins:

  Reach out 1–3 months after treatment ends to see how they're doing. This can reignite engagement or lead to referrals if they know someone else who could benefit from your services.

- Email Newsletters or Updates:

  Send monthly or quarterly newsletters with wellness tips, mental health resources, or announcements about workshops or support groups. This keeps your practice visible and positions you as a trusted resource.

- Seasonal Encouragement Messages:

  Around stressful times (e.g., holidays, back-to-school, or new year), send short encouraging notes. A message like "Remember to take care of yourself this season" can leave a lasting impression.

- Referral Appreciation:

  If a client refers someone to you, express gratitude through a handwritten thank-you card or a simple acknowledgment (while maintaining confidentiality). Appreciation fosters goodwill and encourages continued support.

*****

Final Thoughts

Client engagement is more than just a retention strategy—it's the heartbeat of effective therapy. When clients feel connected, supported, and understood, they are more likely to commit to the process and achieve lasting change.

As a therapist, you have the privilege of walking alongside people in their most vulnerable moments. Every communication, follow-up, and act of kindness deepens that trust. By prioritizing engagement, you not only build a sustainable practice—you build a community of healing, one client at a time.

Chapter 5:

How to Fill Your Practice with Paying Clients

Every therapist dreams of a full, thriving private practice filled with clients who are committed to their healing journey—and who can pay for the value of the services they receive. But creating that reality doesn't happen by chance; it requires a clear strategy, a confident mindset, and consistent action.

In this chapter, we'll explore how to attract and retain paying clients who appreciate your expertise, respect your time, and align with your mission as a healer.

*****

The Power of Specialization

One of the most effective ways to fill your practice is to narrow your focus rather than trying to serve everyone. A common mistake among new therapists is believing that casting a wider net will bring more clients. In reality, specialization attracts clarity—and clarity attracts the right people.

Ask yourself:

- What issues am I most passionate about helping clients overcome?
- What problems do I solve best?
- What types of clients energize and inspire me?

When you specialize, you position yourself as an expert, not just a general therapist. Clients aren't just looking for someone who "does therapy." They're looking for someone who understands their specific pain point deeply.

For example:

- If you specialize in postpartum depression, your messaging, marketing, and website should all speak directly to new mothers struggling with identity and mood changes.
- If you focus on trauma recovery, your content should reflect understanding, safety, and restoration.
- If you help professionals manage anxiety and burnout, tailor your approach toward high-achievers seeking balance.

A clear niche builds trust faster and helps potential clients self-identify as the people you were meant to help.

*****

Communicating the Value of Transformation

People don't buy therapy—they invest in transformation. When communicating about your services, shift the focus from "what you do" to "what changes when clients work with you."

Instead of saying:

"I offer therapy for anxiety and stress management."

Say:

"I help women break free from anxiety so they can feel calm, confident, and in control again."

The second statement paints a picture of outcome, not just service. It communicates the emotional relief and tangible transformation your clients will experience.

When people understand the value of what you offer, they're more willing to pay your worth. They're not just paying for 50 minutes— they're investing in hope, healing, and a better life.

To communicate transformation effectively:

- Use client-centered language ("You'll feel more confident..." rather than "I will help clients...").
- Share success stories or anonymous client journeys (with permission and confidentiality maintained).
- Emphasize the benefits of therapy—clarity, peace, growth, emotional freedom.
- Always link your service to the result clients desire most.

*****

Setting Prices to Reflect Expertise

Your prices communicate your confidence, your value, and your experience. Setting them too low not only undervalues your work but also attracts clients who may not be as committed to the process.

As discussed in Chapter 2, undercharging often comes from fear—fear of rejection, comparison, or not being "good enough." But to build a sustainable practice, you must price in a way that honors your education, expertise, and time.

When setting prices:

1. Know your numbers. Calculate your business expenses, desired income, and the number of clients you can realistically see per week.
2. Consider your market, but don't be ruled by it. Research what similar professionals charge in your area, but remember that you can differentiate through value.
3. Price for commitment. Clients who pay your full rate tend to show up more consistently and take therapy more seriously.
4. Review your pricing annually. As your expertise grows, so should your rates.

Your ideal clients will respect your professionalism and happily pay for the transformation you provide.

*****

Offering Trial Sessions

While you should value your time, offering a limited introductory or consultation session can be a powerful strategy to build connection and trust with new clients.

A short discovery call or reduced-rate initial consultation allows potential clients to:

- Understand your approach and feel safe with your style.
- Ask questions about the therapy process.
- Determine if it's a good fit before committing financially.

This strategy isn't about discounting your value—it's about reducing perceived risk. Once clients experience your warmth and expertise, they're far more likely to commit to ongoing sessions.

To use this effectively:

- Keep the session short (15–20 minutes).
- Set clear boundaries: this is a consultation, not therapy.
- Use the time to explain your process, answer questions, and outline next steps.
- End with a confident invitation:

"If this feels like the right fit for you, I'd love to schedule your first session so we can begin your journey toward healing."

*****

Leveraging Online Directories and Referrals

Online visibility is one of the most powerful tools in modern private practice growth. Potential clients often begin their search for a therapist online, which means you need to show up where they're looking.

Online Directories

Create professional listings on platforms like:

- Psychology Today
- TherapyDen
- Zencare
- GoodTherapy

Make your profile stand out with:

- A warm, inviting headshot
- A clear, compassionate description of your services
- Keywords that reflect your specialty (e.g., "anxiety therapy for women," "Christian counseling," "trauma-informed care")

Referrals

Never underestimate the power of word-of-mouth. Build strong referral relationships with:

- Physicians and psychiatrists
- Schools and universities
- Pastors and faith communities
- Other therapists who serve different niches

Stay top-of-mind by sending thank-you notes, referring clients in return, and maintaining a reputation of professionalism and reliability.

*****

Community Outreach and Content Marketing

Therapists who engage with their community build a loyal following—and loyal followings turn into full caseloads. Visibility builds familiarity, and familiarity builds trust.

Here are ways to connect with your community both locally and online:

1. Host Free Workshops or Webinars.

    Offer educational sessions on topics like stress management, parenting, or self-care. These events showcase your expertise and build relationships with potential clients.

2. Partner with Local Organizations.

    Collaborate with schools, nonprofits, and community centers to provide mental health education. This not only increases visibility but also fulfills your mission of outreach and service.

3. Share Valuable Content Online.

    Create blog posts, podcasts, or short social media videos that address real challenges your audience faces. When you provide consistent, helpful information, people start to see you as their go-to expert.

4. Use Storytelling.

    Share your journey and your "why." Clients resonate with authenticity. When they see your humanity, they feel safe opening up about theirs.

5. Engage Consistently.

    Respond to comments, emails, or inquiries with care and professionalism. Connection leads to conversion—and genuine engagement turns followers into clients.

*****

Final Thoughts

Filling your private practice with paying clients is not about chasing numbers—it's about creating alignment. When you clearly define who you serve, communicate the transformation you provide, and show up consistently in your community, clients will naturally be drawn to your practice.

Remember:

- You are not selling therapy; you are offering healing.
- You are not competing; you are serving a specific need.
- You are not begging for clients; you are inviting transformation.

A full practice is simply a reflection of your clarity, confidence, and commitment to impact. Trust that the right clients will find you when your message, methods, and mindset are aligned with your mission.

Chapter 6:

Trusting the Process

Every therapist, no matter how experienced or skilled, faces seasons of doubt in private practice. You might wonder if your clients are progressing fast enough, if your marketing is working, or if you're truly making an impact. Likewise, clients often question whether therapy is "working" or if healing will ever come.

This chapter reminds both you—and your clients—that trusting the process is essential. Growth rarely happens overnight, but with patience, consistency, and faith, it does happen.

Trusting the process means believing in the power of small steps, steady progress, and the unseen work happening beneath the surface—both in your clients and in your business.

*****

Educating Clients About the Therapy Journey

One of the keys to helping clients trust the process is to educate them early and often about what therapy actually entails. Many clients come in expecting instant relief or quick results, not realizing that transformation takes time and commitment.

At the start of treatment, set the expectation that:

- Healing is not linear. There will be breakthroughs, plateaus, and setbacks.
- Emotional discomfort is often a sign that progress is being made.
- Growth requires patience, consistency, and courage.

You might say:

"Therapy is like training a muscle. The more we work through challenges, the stronger and more resilient you'll become. Some sessions may feel harder than others, but every single one contributes to your overall growth."

When clients understand that their progress may look different from what they imagined, they're less likely to feel discouraged during tough moments.

As a therapist, your calm confidence helps them stay grounded. When they sense that you trust the process, they begin to as well.

*****

Setting Realistic Expectations

Managing expectations—both your own and your clients'—is crucial in maintaining motivation and preventing burnout. Unrealistic goals can create frustration, while realistic ones cultivate hope and perseverance.

For Clients:

Help them define measurable and achievable goals early on. Instead of vague statements like "I want to be happier," encourage more specific, attainable objectives such as:

- "I want to experience fewer panic attacks each week."
- "I want to learn to set boundaries with my family."
- "I want to feel more confident at work."

Breaking goals into small, actionable steps helps clients see tangible progress—even if overall transformation takes time.

For You as the Therapist:

It's equally important to set realistic expectations for your business and yourself. Private practice growth, like therapy, is gradual. You may not fill your schedule immediately or reach your income goals in the first few months—and that's okay.

Trust that your effort, consistency, and quality of care will eventually bear fruit. Every satisfied client, every improved session, and every moment of learning adds to your long-term success.

*****

Building a Strong Therapeutic Alliance

At the core of trusting the process is the therapeutic alliance—the collaborative relationship between therapist and client. Research consistently shows that this alliance is one of the strongest predictors of therapeutic success, regardless of modality or technique.

To build and strengthen this alliance:

1. Foster Safety and Authenticity. Create an environment where clients feel seen, heard, and respected without judgment.
2. Collaborate, Don't Dictate. Empower clients to be active participants in their healing process. Use phrases like, "How does that feel to you?" or "What do you think would help most this week?"
3. Be Transparent. When appropriate, share insights about why you're using a particular approach or technique. Transparency builds trust and deepens engagement.
4. Model Vulnerability and Humanity. Within professional boundaries, being authentic reminds clients that healing is a shared human journey—not a hierarchical exchange.

The therapeutic alliance helps clients stay committed, even when therapy feels challenging. It reassures them that they're not alone on the journey.

*****

Tracking and Celebrating Progress

Progress in therapy is often subtle and gradual. Clients might not always notice how far they've come unless you help them reflect on it.

Integrate progress tracking into your sessions:

- Review treatment goals periodically.
- Use measurable scales (e.g., rating anxiety from 1–10).
- Revisit intake notes to highlight improvements over time.

You might say:

"When we first started, you mentioned that social situations made you anxious to the point of avoiding them. Now, you're attending gatherings again. That's a huge step forward!"

Celebrating progress, even small victories, reinforces the belief that therapy works and encourages continued commitment. It's also deeply fulfilling for you as the therapist—it reminds you of your purpose and impact.

Beyond client outcomes, take time to celebrate your own professional growth. Maybe you learned a new therapeutic technique, improved your documentation system, or successfully managed your practice finances for the quarter. These milestones deserve acknowledgment too.

Success in private practice is not just about numbers—it's about consistency, courage, and compassion in motion.

*****

Addressing Setbacks

Setbacks are inevitable—in therapy and in business. Clients may regress, cancel sessions, or resist change. You might experience slow seasons, client drop-offs, or financial stress. The key is to view setbacks as part of the journey, not as signs of failure.

When Clients Struggle:

- Normalize setbacks. Remind clients that healing often involves revisiting old wounds before true growth can occur.
- Reframe relapses as opportunities for insight.

  "This doesn't mean you're back at square one. It means we've uncovered another layer that needs healing."

- Offer reassurance that progress is not erased by one difficult week or month.

When You Struggle:

- Reflect rather than react. Ask, "What is this season teaching me?"
- Seek supervision, consultation, or therapy for yourself if needed.
- Remember your "why." You chose this work because you believe in transformation—yours and others'.

Setbacks can actually strengthen your practice. They build resilience, deepen empathy, and refine your systems. The lessons learned during difficult times often become the foundation for long-term stability and growth.

*****

Final Thoughts

Trusting the process is both a professional discipline and a spiritual practice. It's the quiet confidence that every session, every client, and every challenge is working together for your greater purpose.

When you trust the process:

- You release the need for perfection and embrace progress.
- You find peace in consistency rather than chaos in comparison.
- You model patience and perseverance to your clients—showing them that healing unfolds in its own divine timing.

Remember, success in private practice isn't measured only by full calendars or large profits. It's measured by the lives touched, the growth witnessed, and the faith you hold in the unseen work of transformation.

Trust that the seeds you've planted—in your clients, your practice, and yourself—are growing, even when you can't yet see the fruit.

Chapter 7:

Setting Prices

Money conversations can be one of the most uncomfortable parts of running a private practice. As therapists, we're trained to help people heal, not necessarily to talk about numbers or negotiate fees. Yet, understanding how to set and maintain fair, sustainable pricing is an essential part of operating a thriving, ethical, and stress-free practice.

Setting your rates is not just about economics — it's about honoring your worth, sustaining your mission, and ensuring that your practice can serve people for years to come.

This chapter will help you navigate the mindset, strategy, and structure behind setting prices confidently and ethically — so you can grow your practice without guilt, fear, or burnout.

*****

The Psychology Behind Pricing

Before you even set a number, it's crucial to address the mindset around money. Many therapists struggle with guilt about charging clients what they're truly worth. You might feel torn between your desire to serve and the need to sustain your business.

But here's the truth:

You cannot pour from an empty cup.

Charging appropriately allows you to show up for clients at your best. It ensures you can afford ongoing education, self-care, high-quality tools, and a stable work environment. Undercharging or overextending yourself doesn't make you more compassionate — it makes you more exhausted.

Reframe pricing as an exchange of value, not a transaction. You're not charging for your time alone — you're charging for:

- Years of education, training, and supervision
- Emotional labor and professional expertise
- The healing environment you provide
- Administrative, insurance, and operational costs

When you understand your true value, setting your price becomes an act of integrity, not greed.

*****

Factors to Consider When Setting Your Rates

Several factors determine what's fair and sustainable for your practice. Let's explore the key considerations:

1. Your Credentials and Experience

Your education, certifications, and years of experience should be reflected in your rate. A newly licensed therapist may charge differently than an APRN with advanced clinical skills, but both should set prices that reflect their value and qualifications.

2. Your Niche and Specialty

If you specialize in trauma recovery, addiction, couples therapy, or psychiatric medication management — areas that require advanced skills — your rates can and should be higher. Specialty expertise adds value.

3. Your Location and Market

Research what other providers in your area and with your level of experience are charging.

If you're in a city like Chesapeake, VA, or surrounding regions, consider local market rates but don't feel confined by them. Clients often pay more for quality care and a personalized therapeutic relationship.

4. Your Business Expenses

List all recurring costs associated with running your practice — rent, software, liability insurance, taxes, marketing, office supplies, billing services, continuing education, and more.

A general rule: your rates should not only cover expenses but also provide a livable, sustainable income after taxes.

5. Your Financial and Lifestyle Goals

How many hours per week do you realistically want to work? How much do you want to earn annually?

For example:

If your goal is $100,000/year and you want to work 48 weeks per year, 25 billable sessions weekly, your average session fee needs to be about $83 per session after taxes and expenses — meaning you'll likely charge $125–$150 to reach that goal sustainably.

These calculations turn emotion into logic. Once you see the math, your price becomes grounded in reason rather than guilt.

*****

Calculating Your Rate: A Simple Formula

Here's a simple formula you can use to determine a starting point:

(Annual Income Goal + Annual Expenses) ÷ (Weeks You Plan to Work × Weekly Client Hours) = Hourly Rate

Example:

- Desired income: $80,000
- Annual expenses: $20,000
- Working 48 weeks/year × 25 client hours/week = 1,200 billable hours

($80,000 + $20,000) ÷ 1,200 = $83.33 per hour (minimum base rate)

From there, you can adjust upward for taxes, savings goals, and profit margin — aiming for a session rate around $125–$150.

The number you land on is not random — it's based on strategy, clarity, and sustainability.

*****

Private Pay vs. Insurance: Finding Your Balance

One of the biggest decisions you'll make in private practice is whether to take insurance or operate privately (cash pay).

Insurance-Based Practice

Pros:

- Easier to attract clients initially
- Provides steady referrals
- Increases accessibility for clients

Cons:

- Lower reimbursement rates
- Delayed payments and billing complexities
- Less control over session length and treatment planning

Private Pay Practice

Pros:

- More freedom, flexibility, and autonomy
- Immediate payment and predictable income
- Freedom to offer specialized services

Cons:

- May require stronger marketing to attract clients
- Can feel uncomfortable at first discussing payment directly

You can also choose a hybrid model, accepting a few insurance panels while gradually transitioning to private pay clients.

Remember: You're allowed to evolve your payment model as your confidence, demand, and brand grow.

*****

Communicating Your Rates with Confidence

Discussing money doesn't have to feel awkward. The key is confidence and clarity.

Here are some scripts you can use:

"My session rate is $150 for a 50-minute session. I accept payment at the time of service. I also offer limited sliding scale options for clients experiencing financial hardship."

"My rate reflects not just our session time but the clinical expertise, preparation, and support I provide between sessions."

You're not apologizing for your rate — you're educating and normalizing the value of professional care.

If a client cannot afford your full rate, you have options:

- Offer a few sliding-scale spots for clients in need.
- Refer them to community agencies or lower-cost therapy options.
- Offer group therapy or shorter sessions as a cost-effective alternative.

Boundaries around your pricing are not barriers — they're signs of respect for your time, your energy, and your mission.

*****

Raising Your Rates

As your skills and experience grow, so should your rates. Yet many therapists fear losing clients by raising prices. The truth is, rate increases are a normal and healthy part of business growth.

A good rule of thumb:

- Review your rates every 12–18 months.
- Provide clients with 30–60 days' notice of any increases.
- Offer current clients the option to stay at their current rate for a limited time as a courtesy.

Sample script:

"Beginning [date], my rate will increase to $160 per session. This adjustment allows me to continue providing high-quality care and expand services to better meet your needs. I value your commitment to this process and wanted to communicate the change early."

Most clients understand — and those who don't may not be the right fit for your evolving practice.

*****

Faith and Finances: Aligning Purpose with Profit

For faith-driven therapists, financial integrity is not about greed — it's about stewardship.

You are entrusted with the responsibility to manage your resources wisely, bless others, and sustain your calling.

Proverbs 13:11 (NIV) reminds us:

"Dishonest money dwindles away, but whoever gathers money little by little makes it grow."

Your pricing is a form of stewardship — ensuring that you can continue to serve, give, and grow in excellence. When your practice is profitable, you can:

- Offer scholarships or pro bono sessions
- Hire team members
- Invest in community programs
- Support your family without financial strain

Charging fairly doesn't diminish your compassion — it multiplies your capacity to impact lives.

*****

Final Thoughts

Setting prices is about more than just numbers; it's about clarity, courage, and alignment with your purpose. When you charge your worth, you model to your clients the same self-respect, boundaries, and self-value you encourage in them.

Don't let guilt dictate your pricing — let wisdom and strategy lead instead.

Your work changes lives. Your expertise matters. And your practice deserves to be profitable, purposeful, and sustainable.

As you continue to level up, remember this truth:

You can serve and succeed at the same time.

Chapter 8:

Creating Multiple Streams of Income as a Therapist

As your private practice begins to thrive, you'll reach a point where your calendar is full — yet your income still feels capped. You may realize that you can only see so many clients before you reach emotional and professional exhaustion.

That's where multiple streams of income come in.

This final chapter is about shifting from the mindset of being "just a clinician" to becoming a clinician-entrepreneur — a professional who uses their expertise, experience, and passion to build sustainable wealth while serving others.

Your skills as a therapist are incredibly valuable. They extend far beyond the therapy room — and the world needs your insight in many different forms.

*****

1. Why Diversifying Your Income Matters

Relying solely on one income source — like one-on-one sessions — can limit your financial growth and increase burnout. Diversifying your income not only stabilizes your finances but also gives you freedom, flexibility, and security.

It allows you to:

- Work smarter, not harder
- Reduce dependence on insurance reimbursements
- Create passive or semi-passive income
- Expand your impact to a wider audience

When you diversify, you transition from surviving session to session — to building a mission-driven brand that generates income even when you're not in the office.

*****

2. Potential Income Streams for Therapists

Below are proven ways therapists, coaches, and mental health professionals can expand their income beyond traditional sessions.

a. Coaching Services

If you're passionate about motivation, mindset, or personal growth, consider offering life or mental wellness coaching.

Coaching differs from therapy — it's future-focused and goal-oriented. You can help clients build confidence, improve relationships, or overcome fear, without diagnosing or treating mental illness.

This can be a powerful addition to your practice, especially for high-functioning clients seeking transformation rather than treatment.

b. Online Courses and Workshops

You can package your expertise into online courses, webinars, or workshops.

Example topics:

- Overcoming Anxiety Naturally
- Boundaries and Burnout Recovery
- Healing from Toxic Relationships
- Mindfulness for Busy Professionals

These offerings can run live or pre-recorded, giving you the freedom to serve many people at once — even while you sleep.

c. Group Therapy or Support Groups

Hosting group sessions allows you to help multiple clients simultaneously while maximizing your income per hour.

It also creates a sense of community and accountability that many clients crave.

For example:

- "Women Healing from Trauma" group
- "Coping with Depression" group
- "Faith and Healing" support group

Groups can be billed at a lower per-person rate but yield higher total revenue than individual sessions.

d. Speaking Engagements and Workshops

You have a story and wisdom that others need to hear. Speaking at conferences, churches, schools, or organizations about topics like mental health awareness, self-care, or resilience can position you as a thought leader and generate additional income.

You can charge speaking fees, sell books, or gain new clients from exposure.

e. Writing a Book or Workbook

Publishing a book allows you to turn your message into a tangible resource that lives beyond the therapy room.

Books like Leveling Up Your Private Practice don't just inform — they build authority, credibility, and passive income. You can expand your written work into:

- Workbooks
- Journals
- Devotionals
- Companion courses

Each piece of content can work together to create a full ecosystem around your message.

f. Digital Products

Digital products are a fantastic source of passive income. You can create:

- E-books
- Downloadable templates (client forms, self-care guides)
- Affirmation cards
- Mental health trackers
- Therapist business planners

Once created, digital products sell repeatedly with minimal ongoing effort.

g. Supervision or Mentorship

If you're licensed at a higher level or have years of experience, you can offer clinical supervision or mentorship to new therapists or psychiatric providers.

Mentorship not only helps shape the next generation of clinicians but also provides a fulfilling and reliable income source.

h. Consulting Services

Many organizations need mental health expertise for staff training, crisis management, or program development. You can become a consultant for schools, nonprofits, corporate teams, or churches.

This work often pays at a higher hourly rate than clinical sessions and expands your professional influence.

i. Affiliate Marketing and Partnerships

If you use or recommend wellness products, apps, or professional tools, you can partner with those brands through affiliate programs — earning a small commission from your recommendations.

This works best when you authentically share tools that align with your practice values.

*****

3. Adding Clinical and Integrative Services to Your Practice

As you grow in your career and expand your private practice, you'll discover that your income and impact don't have to be limited to traditional therapy sessions. You are a mental health professional with deep clinical knowledge, and the world of integrative wellness, mental health innovation, and holistic healing is expanding rapidly.

In addition to courses, coaching, writing, consulting, and digital products, you also have the opportunity to expand your clinical offerings in ways that enhance patient outcomes and diversify your revenue.

Many therapists and psychiatric providers today are building hybrid practices that blend mental health with functional wellness, integrative medicine, and innovative treatments. By doing so, they not only differentiate their practice but provide clients with whole-person healing.

Below is a powerful section detailing how you can add high-impact clinical services — legally, ethically, and profitably — to your practice.

The landscape of mental health care is evolving, and clients now seek practitioners who can offer comprehensive mental, physical, and emotional healing options. By incorporating additional clinical services into your private practice, you can:

- Increase revenue streams
- Improve patient outcomes
- Provide personalized and innovative care
- Stand out in a saturated market
- Address root causes of mental health challenges, not just symptoms

Here are six powerful modalities you can incorporate to elevate your practice to a full-spectrum healing center.

A. Vitamins — Including NAD — to Correct Deficiencies

Vitamin supplementation has become a cornerstone of holistic psychiatric care. Research consistently shows that deficiencies in vitamins, minerals, and amino acids can significantly impact mood, energy levels, cognitive function, and emotional regulation.

Why It Matters

Many psychiatric symptoms mimic deficiency symptoms. For example:

- Low B12 can cause fatigue and depression
- Vitamin D deficiency can mimic anxiety and low mood
- Magnesium deficiency contributes to insomnia and irritability

By incorporating nutritional testing and vitamin supplementation, you help clients heal from the inside out.

NAD (Nicotinamide Adenine Dinucleotide)

NAD therapy is gaining nationwide attention for its ability to support:

- Cellular repair
- Brain functioning
- Mental clarity
- Addiction recovery
- Chronic stress and burnout

You can offer NAD in the form of:

- IV infusions
- IM injections
- Sublingual supplements

This service is high-value, in-demand, and profitable.

*****

B. Infusions (IV Therapy)

IV infusion therapy brings medical-level wellness directly into private practice. It allows clients to receive potent nutrients directly into the bloodstream, bypassing digestive issues and offering rapid symptom relief.

Common IV Infusions

- Hydration therapy
- Vitamin C
- B-complex and B12
- Magnesium
- NAD
- Anxiety and stress relief blends
- Immunity boosting blends

Benefits to Clients

- Enhanced mood
- Improved energy
- Faster recovery from fatigue

- Relief during depressive episodes
- Faster cognitive clarity

Benefits to Your Practice

IV therapy is one of the fastest-growing wellness services, and clients often return weekly or monthly — giving your practice steady recurring revenue.

*****

C. Ketamine Therapy

Ketamine has revolutionized psychiatric care, offering relief to clients who have not improved with traditional medications or therapy alone.

Why It's Powerful

Ketamine helps with:

- Treatment-resistant depression
- PTSD
- Suicidal thoughts
- Anxiety
- Chronic stress
- Emotional trauma

It works by rapidly increasing neuroplasticity — helping the brain create new pathways for healing.

Service Models

You can offer:

- Ketamine infusions
- Ketamine-assisted psychotherapy (KAP)
- Ketamine lozenges (oral)

Integrative Opportunity

Many therapists pair ketamine sessions with deep psychotherapy, making it a powerful way to accelerate healing and breakthroughs.

*****

D. Psychedelic-Assisted Therapies

As psychedelic legalization progresses across states, practitioners are preparing to integrate therapeutic modalities using substances such as:

- Psilocybin
- MDMA
- Future FDA-approved psychedelics

Why This Matters

Psychedelic therapy is poised to become one of the biggest mental health revolutions of our time. These therapies have shown promising results for:

- Trauma
- Depression
- Anxiety
- Addiction
- Identity healing
- End-of-life support

Your Role

Even before legalization, providers can begin preparing by offering:

- Psychedelic integration therapy
- Pre- and post-journey counseling
- Educational workshops

When fully legal, practitioners who are already trained will be ahead of the industry curve.

*****

E. Hormone Replacement Therapy (HRT)

Hormone imbalances can directly affect mental health, including:

- Depression
- Anxiety
- Insomnia
- Fatigue
- Weight gain
- Mood swings

- Low libido
- Cognitive fog

As a psychiatric APRN or therapist collaborating with medical professionals, you can incorporate:

HRT Options

- Thyroid optimization
- Testosterone replacement therapy
- Estrogen and progesterone balancing
- Bioidentical hormone replacement

Why Add It to Your Practice?

Mental health and hormonal health are deeply connected. Integrating these services makes your practice a one-stop solution for mind-body wellness.

*****

F. Holistic Massages

Holistic massage therapy is more than relaxation—it's a therapeutic intervention for mental, emotional, and physical well-being.

Types of Massage You Can Integrate

- Trauma-informed massage
- Lymphatic drainage

- Craniosacral therapy
- Deep tissue
- Aromatherapy
- Holistic wellness massage

Benefits to Clients

- Regulates the nervous system
- Reduces anxiety and stress
- Supports trauma recovery
- Improves sleep
- Releases somatic tension
- Complements therapy beautifully

Benefits to Your Practice

Adding a licensed massage therapist to your team creates:

- Passive income
- Additional client services
- Holistic mind-body healing options

Holistic massage services contribute to a truly integrative mental health center.

*****

Why These Services Transform Your Practice

Adding these clinical and wellness services allows you to:

✔ Offer whole-person care

✔ Create multiple income streams

✔ Attract high-paying, high-commitment clients

✔ Increase your practice value and demand

✔ Stand out as a psychiatric provider offering next-level care

You become not just a therapist — but a wellness innovator, a clinical leader, and a transformational healer in your community.

*****

4. The Power of Systems and Automation

As you diversify, time management becomes essential.

To keep your business efficient, consider implementing systems that handle repetitive tasks automatically:

- Client management platforms for scheduling, billing, and documentation (e.g., SimplePractice, TherapyNotes).
- Email automation tools for newsletters and marketing.
- Online course platforms like Kajabi, Teachable, or Thinkific.

Automation allows you to focus on creativity and client care while technology handles the rest.

*****

5. Financial Planning for Long-Term Success

With multiple income streams, it's important to organize your finances strategically.

Here's how to stay on track:

- Separate business and personal accounts to maintain clarity.
- Hire a tax professional who understands therapy practices.
- Budget for reinvestment — put money back into marketing, education, and automation tools.
- Build an emergency fund to sustain your practice during slow seasons.

Your goal is to create a business that thrives in both abundance and uncertainty.

*****

6. Legacy and Longevity

Building wealth as a therapist isn't about greed — it's about legacy.

You're not just creating income for yourself; you're creating impact that outlives your sessions.

Think beyond your office:

- How can your brand continue to change lives 10 years from now?
- What systems or resources can you leave behind for future therapists or clients?

- How can your story inspire others to build with both heart and strategy?

You are the architect of your legacy. Every step you take toward financial independence and business growth multiplies your ability to serve — not just in therapy, but in your community and your calling.

*****

7. Faith, Purpose, and Prosperity

As a faith-driven professional, it's important to remember:

You are not just building a practice — you are building purpose.

Deuteronomy 8:18 reminds us,

"But remember the Lord your God, for it is he who gives you the ability to produce wealth."

Your ability to earn, innovate, and expand your reach is a divine gift. Prosperity, when aligned with purpose, becomes ministry.

Through your business, you're not only helping clients heal — you're modeling what it looks like to walk in faith, excellence, and abundance.

*****

Final Words of Encouragement

Leveling up your private practice is more than a professional journey — it's a personal transformation.

You've learned how to:

- Charge your worth
- Protect your time
- Market with confidence
- Engage and retain clients
- Fill your practice intentionally
- Trust the process
- Price with clarity
- Expand with purpose

Now, it's time to step boldly into the next level — where your passion meets profit, and your mission fuels a movement.

Remember this truth:

You were never called to play small. You were called to serve greatly, lead boldly, and prosper with integrity. Your practice is a reflection of your purpose — and your purpose is powerful. Keep leveling up, one step of faith at a time.

Conclusion:

Stepping Into the Next Level of Your Practice

If you've made it to this point, one thing is clear—you are no longer thinking about private practice the same way you once did. You've shifted from simply wanting to help people to understanding that how you build your practice matters just as much as who you serve.

Private practice is not just a career path. It is a calling that requires courage, clarity, and commitment. Throughout this book, you've explored what it truly means to run a practice that honors your clinical expertise and your personal well-being. You've confronted uncomfortable truths about undercharging, weak boundaries, inconsistent marketing, and burnout—and you've been given the tools to do something about them.

This is where intention meets action.

*****

You Are More Than a Clinician

One of the most important mindset shifts you can take away from this book is this:

You are not "just" a therapist or Psychiatric NP.

You are a leader, a business owner, and a steward of healing.

Your license allows you to practice—but your vision determines how far you can go.

When you embrace your role as both a healer and an entrepreneur, you give yourself permission to build systems that support your life instead of draining it. You stop apologizing for your rates. You stop second-guessing your boundaries. You stop shrinking your expertise to make others comfortable.

And in doing so, you model confidence, self-respect, and sustainability—for your clients and for the profession as a whole.

*****

Confidence Changes Everything

Confidence doesn't come from perfection. It comes from clarity.

When you:

- Know your worth
- Understand your numbers
- Communicate your value
- Enforce your policies
- Market with intention
- Trust the process

You begin to operate from a place of authority rather than fear.

Clients feel it. Referrers respect it. And your practice responds to it.

Confidence is not arrogance—it is alignment. It is the quiet knowing that you belong in this space and that your work has value beyond measure.

*****

Growth Requires Consistency, Not Comparison

There will always be someone charging more, posting more, or growing faster. But comparison will never build your practice—consistency will.

Stay committed to:

- Showing up even when results are slow
- Refining systems instead of abandoning them
- Learning from setbacks instead of fearing them
- Trusting your pace instead of rushing your purpose

The most sustainable practices are not built overnight. They are built brick by brick—with integrity, patience, and persistence.

*****

Your Practice Is Allowed to Evolve

You are not required to stay where you started.

You are allowed to:

- Change your pricing
- Shift your niche
- Add new services
- Reduce your caseload
- Expand into holistic or integrative care
- Build multiple streams of income

Growth does not mean you've failed—it means you've learned.

As your skills expand, your practice should reflect that evolution. Let your business grow alongside your wisdom.

*****

Impact and Income Can Coexist

Serving others does not require self-sacrifice to the point of depletion.

You can be compassionate and profitable.

You can be ethical and abundant.

You can be faith-driven and financially empowered.

In fact, when your practice is healthy, you are able to:

- Show up fully for your clients
- Invest in your own wellness
- Expand access through education and outreach
- Create long-term impact without burnout

Sustainability is not selfish—it is responsible.

*****

Your Next Step Starts Now

You don't need another certification to begin applying what you've learned here. You don't need permission to implement better boundaries or raise your rates. You don't need to wait until everything feels perfect. You simply need to take the next aligned step.

Whether that step is:

- Revising your policies
- Clarifying your niche
- Updating your website
- Investing in marketing
- Exploring integrative services
- Or trusting yourself more deeply

Take it.

Progress begins the moment you decide that your practice deserves the same care and intention that you give your clients.

*****

Final Words

This book was never about creating a "perfect" practice. It was about helping you build a purposeful, profitable, and sustainable one—on your terms.

You have the knowledge.

You have the credentials.

You have the heart.

Now it's time to lead with confidence. Don't just open a private practice.

Level it up!

Below are some tools to help you along:

Mindset and Motivation Tools

Affirmations for Therapists:

- "I am skilled, capable, and worthy of my fees."
- "My time, energy, and expertise are valuable."
- "I attract clients who respect and invest in their healing."
- "Every challenge is an opportunity to grow my practice and myself."
- "I serve with compassion, confidence, and clarity."

Encourage clients and yourself to read aloud these affirmations daily to maintain focus and confidence.

Self-Care Checklist

Prevent burnout and maintain peak performance:

- Schedule regular breaks between sessions
- Daily mindfulness or meditation practice
- Exercise and physical wellness
- Peer or professional supervision
- Spiritual or reflective practices
- Ongoing continuing education

Encouragement for Implementation

Implementation is where most therapists struggle. Knowledge alone won't grow your practice — action does.

Here are strategies to keep yourself motivated:

1. Set Weekly Goals

Identify one or two actions each week — e.g., updating your website, contacting referral sources, or hosting a workshop.

2. Track Your Wins

Celebrate every new client, referral, or completed session. Recognize progress to reinforce momentum.

3. Develop an Accountability System

Work with a mentor, colleague, or accountability partner to keep yourself on track.

4. Reflect and Adjust

Use your worksheets and trackers to evaluate what's working. Adjust your strategies rather than giving up when things don't go as planned.

5. Keep Your Purpose at the Center

Your mission is bigger than your challenges. Every client you help, every system you refine, and every step you take matters. Remember why you began this journey and let it fuel your persistence.

Additional Resources

Congratulations! You've journeyed through the steps, strategies, and mindset shifts necessary to create a thriving private practice. Now it's time to put these concepts into action.

This chapter provides practical resources that allow you to take action immediately—from client management to self-reflection, pricing, marketing, and personal growth. Think of these tools as your "launchpad" for success.

*****

1. Worksheets Ideas for Client Engagement and Retention

Client Intake Checklist

Ensure every new client begins therapy with clarity and consistency:

- Personal information and contact details
- Insurance or payment information
- Presenting concerns and goals
- Consent forms and HIPAA agreements
- Emergency contacts
- Session expectations and policies

Session Reflection Worksheet

Help clients track their progress between sessions:

- What was most helpful in today's session?
- Key takeaways or insights
- Actions to implement before the next session
- Emotional rating (1–10 scale) for the week
- Challenges faced and coping strategies

Client Follow-Up Tracker

Keep communication consistent to boost engagement:

- Last session date
- Next scheduled session
- Notes for check-ins
- Referral opportunities
- Special milestones to celebrate

*****

2. Create Templates for Practice Management

No-Show and Late Policy Template

Clearly communicate your policies to clients:

- Fee structure for missed or late sessions
- Cancellation deadlines
- Steps for rescheduling
- Contact methods for urgent communication

Pricing and Package Templates

Simplify your offerings for private pay clients:

- Single session rates
- Package deals (e.g., 5 or 10 sessions)
- Sliding scale guidelines
- Refund or rescheduling policies

Marketing & Social Media Planner

Stay consistent and strategic:

- Weekly content goals
- Monthly promotions or workshops
- Social media post ideas
- Email campaigns
- Referral partnerships

*****

3. Financial Planning Resource Ideas

Budgeting Template for Therapists

Track income, expenses, and savings goals:

- Fixed expenses (rent, insurance, software)
- Variable expenses (marketing, office supplies)
- Taxes and professional dues
- Savings and investments
- Profit margins

Rate Calculation Worksheet

Quickly determine what to charge based on income goals and client load:

- Annual income target
- Weekly client hours
- Expenses
- Minimum session fee
- Target session fee

*****

4. Suggested Additional Resources

To continue growing, consider exploring:

- Online Platforms:
    - YourPsychOnDemand.com
    - FreedomFromYourNarcissist.com
    - Cognifulmind.com

- Social Media Platforms:
    - TikTok: www.tiktok.com/@ginat38
    - FB: https://www.facebook.com/gina.twumasi.54?mibextid=LQQJ4d
    - IG: https://instagram.com/gina_the_mind_expert_?igshid=NTc4MTIwNjQ2YQ==

- o YouTube: Psych On DemandGH - YouTube

- Professional Organizations:
    - o American Psychiatric Nurses Association (APNA)
    - o American Psychological Association (APA)
    - o Local state therapy associations for networking and supervision

*****

Final Words of Encouragement

Your journey toward a thriving private practice is a marathon, not a sprint. The tools in this chapter are designed to give you a practical roadmap, reduce overwhelm, and empower you to take intentional steps toward success.

Remember:

- Success comes from clarity, courage, and consistency.
- Your work is valuable, impactful, and deeply needed.
- Every small action compounds over time — leading to a thriving practice, fulfilled clients, and financial freedom.

As you implement these strategies, templates, and worksheets, keep this guiding principle at the forefront:

Your purpose, your passion, and your expertise are the foundation of your success. Trust yourself, trust the process, and trust the impact you are creating.

With faith, strategy, and dedication, your private practice can thrive — transforming lives, including your own.